The Adventures
of Aryan & Ajax

Aryan Currimbhoy

BLUEROSE PUBLISHERS
India | U.K.

Copyright © Aryan Currimbhoy 2025

All rights reserved by author. No part of this publication may be reproduced, stored in a retrieval system or transmitted in any form or by any means, electronic, mechanical, photocopying, recording or otherwise, without the prior permission of the author. Although every precaution has been taken to verify the accuracy of the information contained herein, the publisher assumes no responsibility for any errors or omissions. No liability is assumed for damages that may result from the use of information contained within.

BlueRose Publishers takes no responsibility for any damages, losses, or liabilities that may arise from the use or misuse of the information, products, or services provided in this publication.

For permissions requests or inquiries regarding this publication,
please contact:

BLUEROSE PUBLISHERS
www.BlueRoseONE.com
info@bluerosepublishers.com
+91 8882 898 898
+4407342408967

ISBN: 978-93-5989-609-0

Cover Design: Himanshi
Illustrator: Himanshi
Typesetting: Pooja Sharma

First Edition: March 2025

1

Aryan was bored one day, and he was looking for an adventure. So, he asked his mom to take him for a drive by the ocean. There, Aryan spotted a boat, and thought, here's my chance! He sneakily slipped off on one where there was a sailor. Aryan asked him to go to sea but the sailor said that the seas were too rough. Disappointed, Aryan got off the boat. Just as he was making his way back to his mum, a tall man tapped him on the shoulder. 'I'll sail for you,' said the man to Aryan. Puzzled, Aryan asked him, 'Who are you?' 'I'm an adventurer,' the man said with a smile. And so they set sail.

2

Once at sea, Aryan realised that the sailor had been right. A big storm came, and a huge wave swept the boat 1000 miles south! They swirled through the ocean at rough speed. The force of the wave had cracked the boat. If that weren't bad enough, lightning struck the boat and smashed it to pieces. Aryan and the adventurer held on to floating pieces of wood, and eventually washed up to a gigantic island. That is when he finally got a good look at the adventurer. He had a scar on one eye, ripped sleeves, a gun, and a pocket knife.

3

The island was eerily quiet. Aryan took a few steps forward, wanting to explore the place. A cluster of trees stood before him. I should climb a tree, he thought. Just then, a dragon rose from behind those trees. Immediately, the adventurer pulled out his AK 47 and started shooting. But it was no match for the dragon! The adventurer yelled "RUN!!!" and the two of them ran for cover. 'Look there,' the adventurer pointed to a cave. They dove inside it. The dragon followed them and swooped down before the cave. It tried and tried its best to get inside but couldn't. Defeated, the dragon gave up. But as he flew away his huge wing hit a rock that rolled down in front of the cave.

4

The adventurer and Aryan were now trapped inside. "Well kid, we have to explore this cave and find another way out of here," the adventurer said. Aryan nodded enthusiastically, panting. This was turning out to be a real adventure-the kind he used to read about in story books. Except now he was the hero. It was pitch dark inside. The adventurer took out a large candle from his satchel and lit it. They walked beside each other, going deeper and deeper into the cave. Suddenly, they heard noises. They stopped dead in their tracks. Was there going to be another surprise? Beyond where they were standing, they spotted a group of people. Aryan asked, 'Who are they?' The adventurer didn't answer. He calmly walked up to the group and got a good look at them. 'It seems to be some kind of tribe,' he told Aryan.

5

The tribe members looked angry to see them and knocked them out. When they woke up, Aryan and the adventurer found themselves tied up with thick ropes. The chieftain of the tribe asked them what they were doing on their island. The adventurer explained that they had set off at sea, looking for an adventure but while they were sailing they lost their boat in a huge storm. We are now stranded on t your island Chief'. After hearing the story, the chieftain nodded. The tribe looked at the chieftain, waiting for his approval. Finally, he lifted his hand and said 'O.K!' The rest of the tribe raised their hands and Aryan and the Adventurer were untied.

6

Aryan and the adventurer were led by the Chieftain to a bamboo hut with tables laden with tropical fruits. Aryan was hungry by now and he quickly picked up one and munched on it. The tribesmen now looked friendly. The Adventurer asked them why they were living in this cave. The chieftain explained that they were a peaceful tribe. Then one day, their island was ravaged by a dragon! An enormous red dragon. Aryan immediately recognised that it was the same dragon that chased them. 'Many died, but the rest of us hid in this cave. Everyday two of us go outside at night in pairs to collect food, water, and materials for weapons. We have learned that the best materials we can get for weapons are dragon scales.'

7

'We succeeded in getting some only a few times. But it is dangerous. One of the two members who go out always die, except for one time when both survived,' the chieftain explained. He asked Aryan and the adventurer if they could try to get some dragon scales. Before Aryan could reply, the Adventurer said, "Sure!" Aryan gaped at him but didn't argue. He was looking for an adventure but this was getting too dangerous for him. The adventurer enquired if they could keep some dragon scales as weapons to fight the dragon. The chieftain agreed but said they must return the scales once they were back. Then, he disappeared farther into the cave for about two minutes, returning with a bow and arrows and some strange tribal weapons.

8

Aryan and the Adventurer lifted the weapons. The tip of the arrow had red scales on it. There was a spear with scales on the tip, and a sword with scales on the blade. Well equipped, Aryan and the Adventurer set out in the night on their quest. Aryan realised that he never got a chance to ask the Adventurer his name. The Adventurer responded, 'People call me Ajax the Adventurer.' What a cool name,' Aryan thought. As they trudged along talking in hushed tones, suddenly a wolf jumped out of some bushes. It looked exactly like the hound of Passarella's but Ajax was quick and so was Aryan. Ajax fired the bow and Aryan chopped his head off with the sword. Phew, they sighed! That was close.

9

But there was more danger lying ahead. Aryan and Ajax were stunned when another big wolf came up behind them and attacked fiercely. Ajax remembered from some of his adventures that wolves travelled in packs. In a flash, another big wolf jumped up from behind them. Ajax fired off arrows, hitting the wolf's paw. The wolf fell at their feet, his paw bleeding. The pack emerged. Twelve more wolves surrounded them. Each one was as big as the hound of Passarella's. Then a great idea struck Ajax! He pulled a steak out of his bag. Aryan looked on in amazement. 'Why are you carrying steaks?' he asked Ajax, thoroughly confused. 'It's a supply for emergencies like this,' Ajax shrugged.

10

Ajax flung a bunch of steaks aiming directly ay the pack of wolves. One of the pieces went and hit a wolf smack in the face. It growled. But just then, another wolf leapt up from behind and pounced on the steak, devouring it hungrily. Seeing this Ajax threw a dozen more. They watched the pack of wolves devour them until the last bit. This seemed to have worked well. After the wolves had devoured the steaks, they pounced on Aryan and Ajax. The two were stunned by this and ducked behind but instead of attacking them, the pack licked them and wagged their tails! As if a light bulb had been turned on, Ajax got another idea.

11

'I have a plan that will defeat the dragon and make this Island peaceful again', said Ajax. The tribe looked confused. Ajax explained that they were ambushed by the pack of wolves but after taming them they could now use them to defeat the dragon. The Chieftain said it could be dangerous with only one pack of wolves but if they had an army of them and some dragon scales they could win. Aryan added that this was a good plan but to defeat the dragon they would have to keep repeating what they did tonight over and over again to get the wolves trained.

12

The next night Aryan and Ajax made a plan to build an army of wolves. It was cloudy and dark so they could remain hidden. They went deep into the forest, got ambushed, and before the wolves could kill them, they gave them food and tamed them. Each time the wolves seemed a little friendlier. They repeated the process. Days passed, weeks passed, a few months and finally one year passed. After repeated training sessions, the wolves learned how to work together and pounce at the right time. They were also taught to pounce at the weak points of the dragon.

13

And so, it was finally time. The tyranny of the dragon would end if the plan was a success. The tribe would finally get its island back. Aryan and Ajax along with the tribesmen lead their army of wolves to defeat the big dragon. Everyone was on edge, but the wolves around them were not. They looked as if it was a regular day of hunting. They walked around in the dense jungle for twenty-five minutes, looking for the dragon. Luckily, it was asleep. All was quiet. Suddenly, there was a whooshing sound. One of the dragon's eyes snapped open, followed by the other. This was it. It was showtime!

14

The dragon rose. It looked much bigger than it was the first time. There was silence. The dragon snorted a couple of times, fumes coming out of its nostrils. Then out of his mouth it breathed out a great big stream of fire. Everyone ran for their lives! Ajax fired his arrows, but the fire just burnt them to ash. Then the wolves pounced, biting his neck and tail which were its weak points. The dragon growled angrily. At first, the tribe was astonished at the wolves just leaping onto the huge dragon. But seeing their courage they rushed to help the wolves hitting, kicking, and trying to slay the dragon.

15

The dragon roared now with all its might. That roar could be heard all through the island. The earth beneath their feet shook. The battle raged on. A tribe and their wolves versus the mighty dragon. After a while, they heard a strange sound that seemed like thunder. Ajax and Aryan looked for the source of the sound. The tribesmen stopped what they were doing too, confused. Everyone turned towards the dragon. The dragon stood still, unsure of what to do. After a minute or so, they all saw what was causing the noise!

16

It was more animals! Tigers, bears, foxes—the entire jungle community had joined in! All heard the cry of the dragon. They came to kill it because the cry said it was weak. They wanted to help the tribe and the wolves. Ajax and Aryan pounced on the dragon, helping the tribe, followed by the entire jungle. It could have lasted days, but it took approximately ten minutes to finish the battle because the jungle had come together and fought as one. The animals and the tribe had won the battle led by Ajax and Aryan and the jungle was finally free of the big red dragon!

17

It was time to return but Aryan and Ajax spotted something in the cave. Everyone was curious about what it was, but the wolves seemed to know. They went inside and pulled out a chest full of treasures. Inside there was gold, diamonds, rubies, and precious gems! The wolves gifted the treasure box to Aryan and Ajax. They then motioned to them to come to the end of the cave. Something else was there. Huddled together, they found baby dragons opening their eyes. Aryan and Ajax smiled at them. They told the wolves to treat them like their own and make them friendly so they could all live together. Then they said goodbye, but before they left, they took the treasure along. At home, they split it fifty-fifty. Aryan hoped he would see Ajax again. What an adventure it had been!

www.ingramcontent.com/pod-product-compliance
Lightning Source LLC
LaVergne TN
LVHW061627070526
838199LV00070B/6613